CONTEST WINNERS FOR TWO

0 Original Piano Duets from the Alfred, Belwin, and Myklas Libraries

Foreword

Exciting piano duets are motivating for students, as well as thrilling for audiences. Thoughtfully written and carefully graded original duets are essential for every piano studio and produce successful learning experiences for students.

Over the years Alfred, Belwin, and Myklas produced an extensive catalogue of quality elementary and intermediate supplementary piano duets. The pieces that are included in this volume represent the three companies' most popular and effective duets drawn from festival and contest lists. Divided into five graded collections, outstanding works are made available again by Dennis Alexander, Dick Averre, Melody Bober, David Carr Glover, David Karp, Carrie Kraft, Ernest J. Kramer, Sharon Lohse Kunitz, Kathleen Massoud, Carol Matz, Shirley Mier, Ruth Perdew, John Robert Poe, Catherine Rollin, Michael Shott, Robert D. Vandall, Judy East Wells, and Carol Wickham. Their time-tested duets are found on the following pages in approximate order of difficulty.

Contents

Produced by
Alfred Music
P.O. Box 10003
Van Nuys, CA 91410-0003
alfred.com

ISBN-10: 0-7390-9971-X
ISBN-13: 978-0-7390-9971-1

REMEMBER WHEN

SECONDO

Robert D. Vandall

Rhythmic (♩. = 60–72)

p

5

no pedal

REMEMBER WHEN

PRIMO

Robert D. Vandall

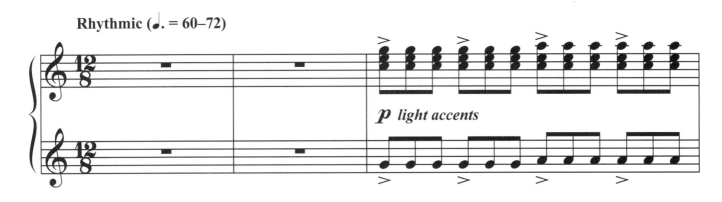

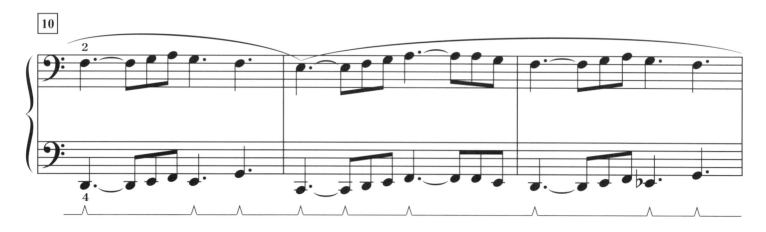

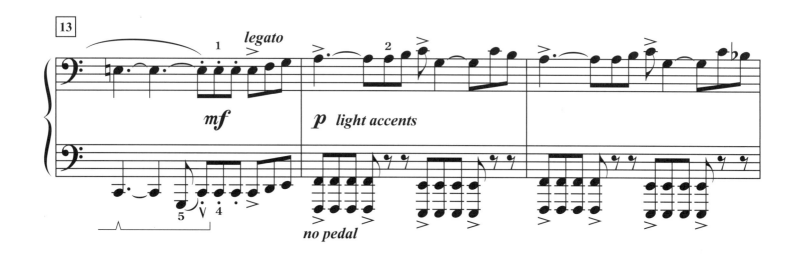

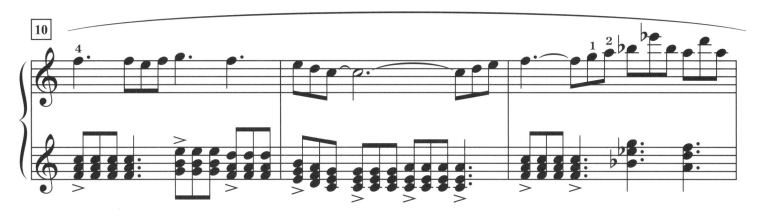

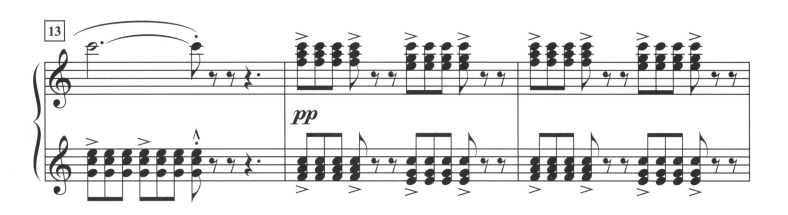

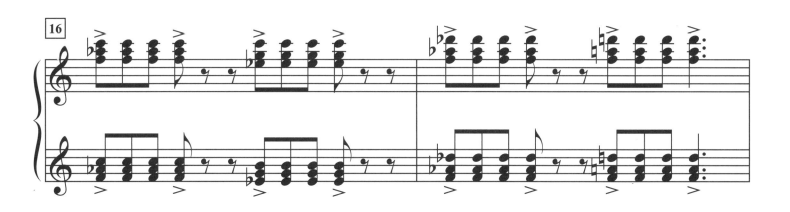

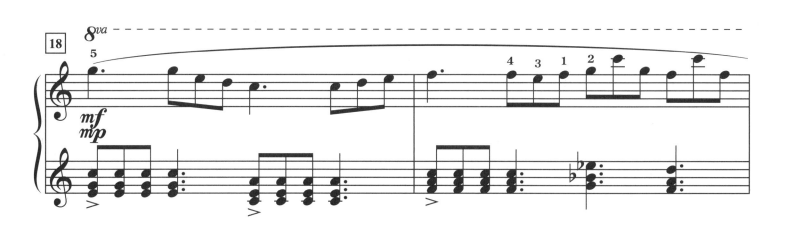

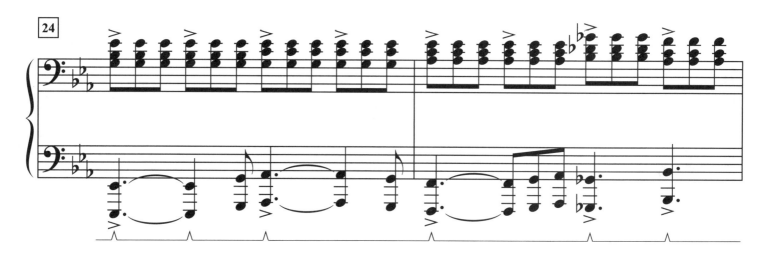

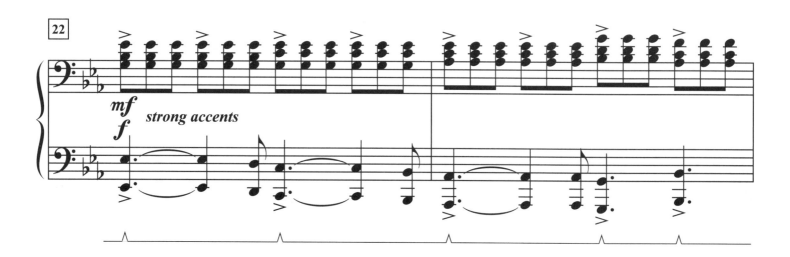

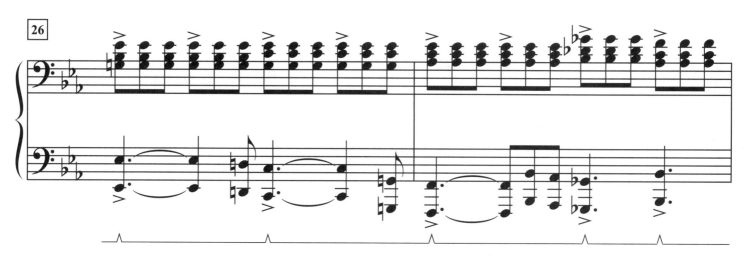

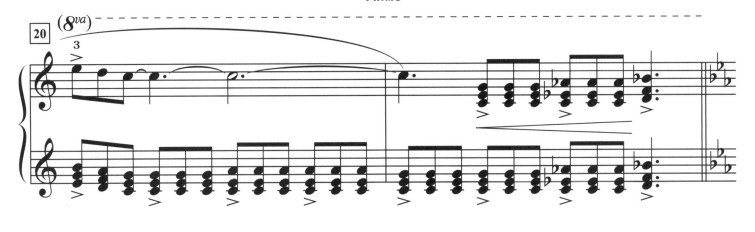

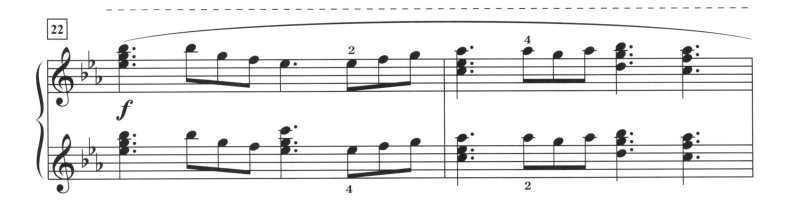

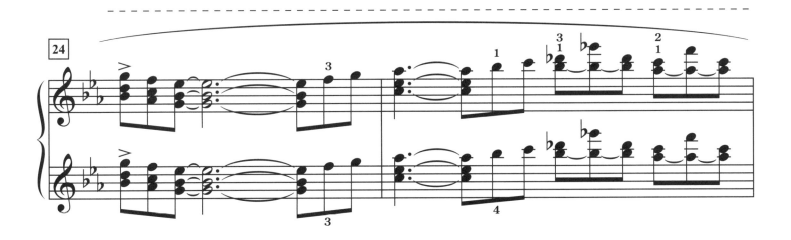

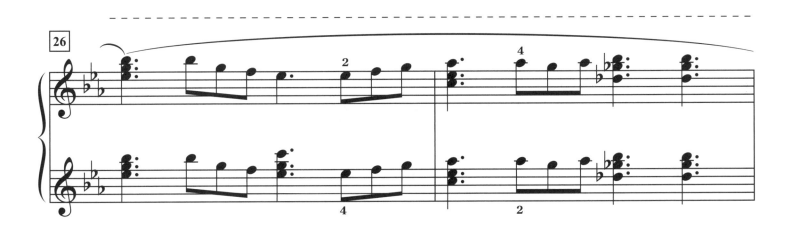

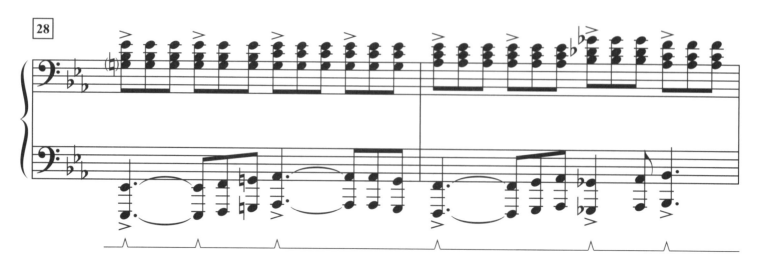

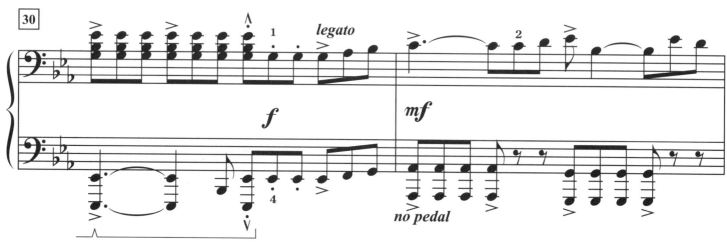

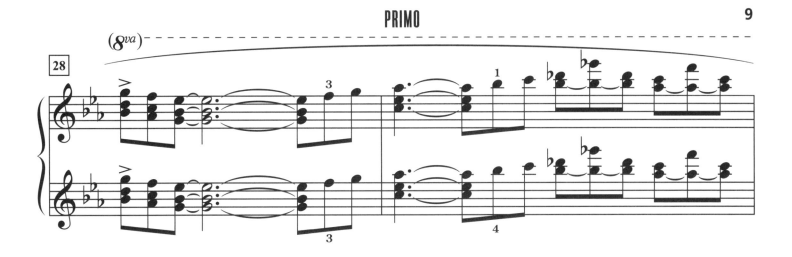

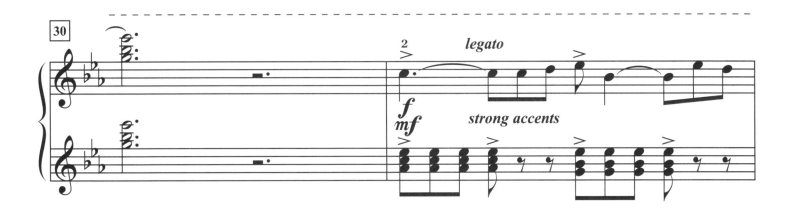

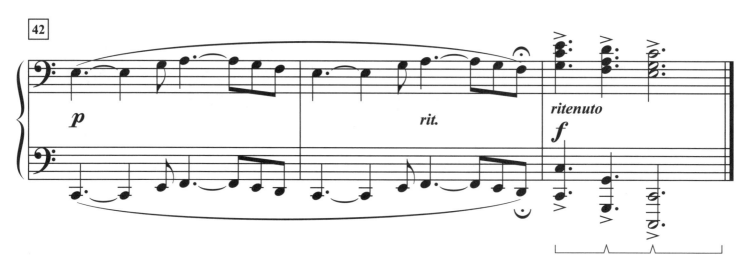

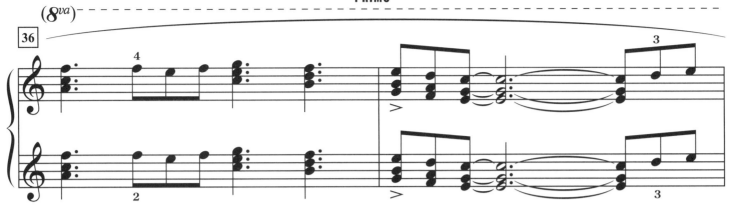

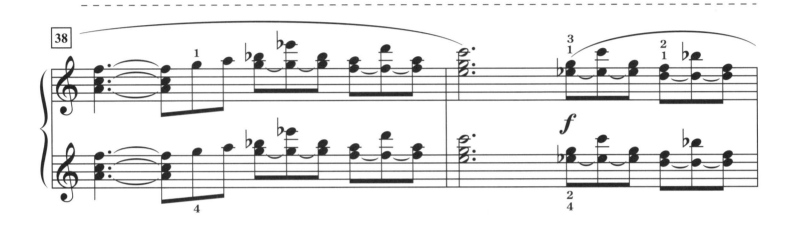

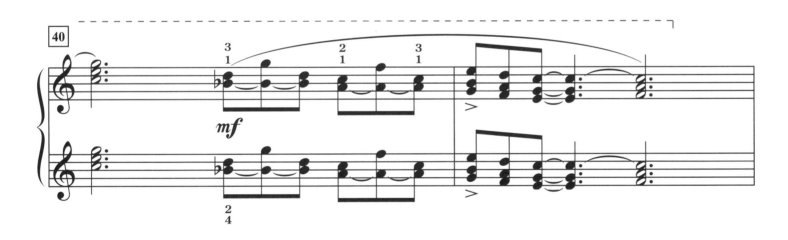

For Dr. Lucien Stark

KANSAS CITY RAG

SECONDO

Ernest J. Kramer

For Dr. Lucien Stark

KANSAS CITY RAG

PRIMO

Ernest J. Kramer

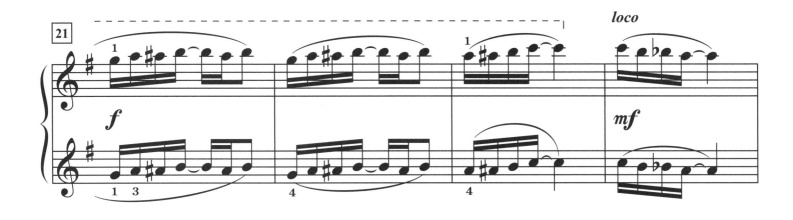

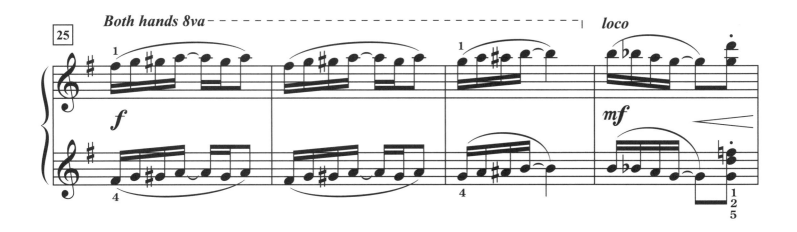

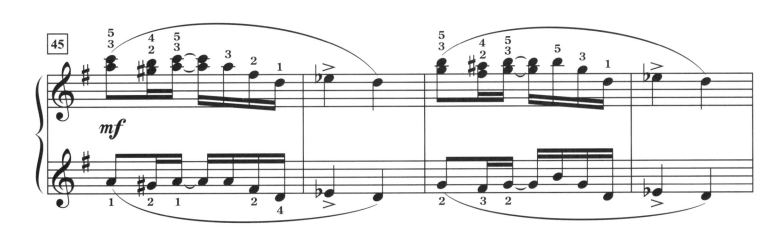

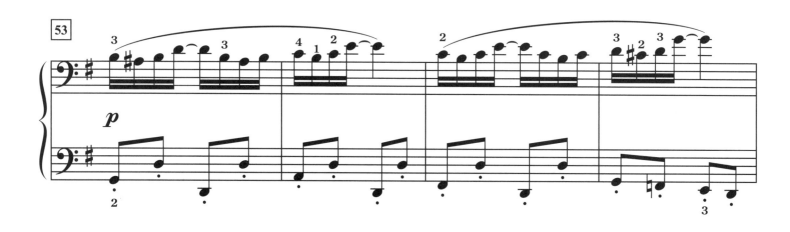

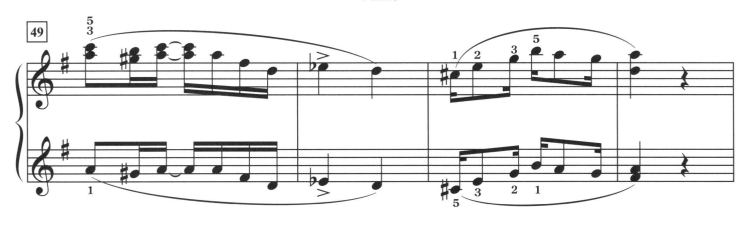

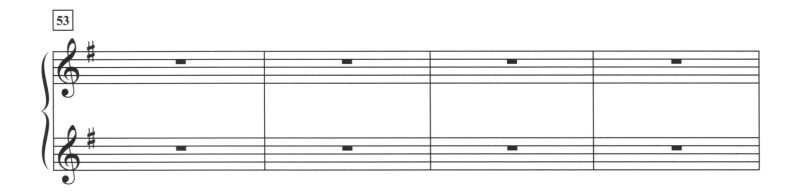

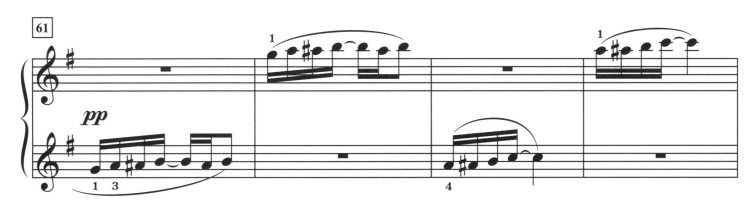

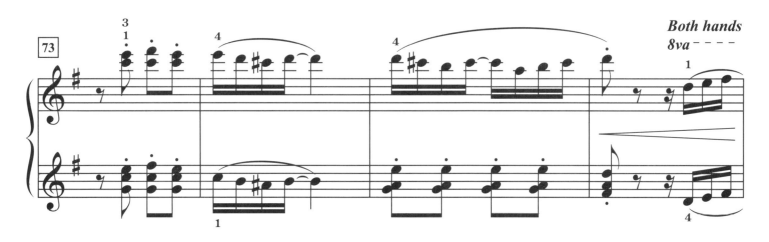

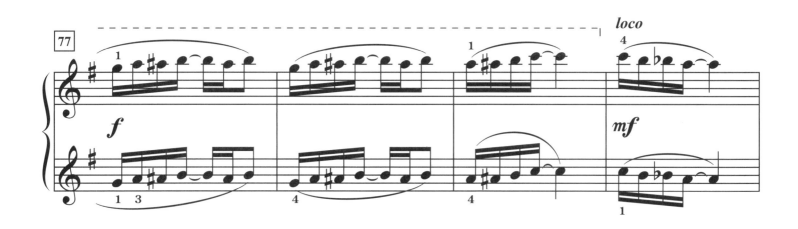

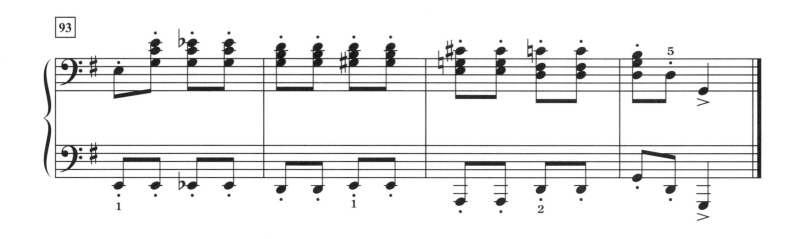

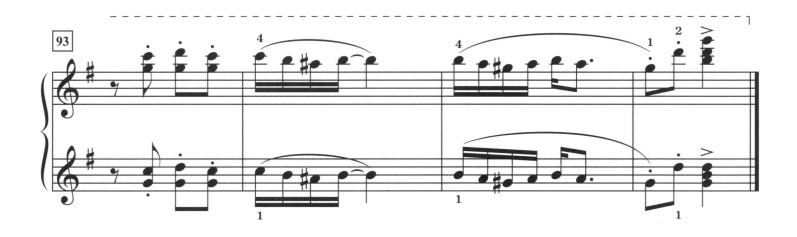

To Karen

THREE WALTZES

1.

SECONDO

Robert D. Vandall

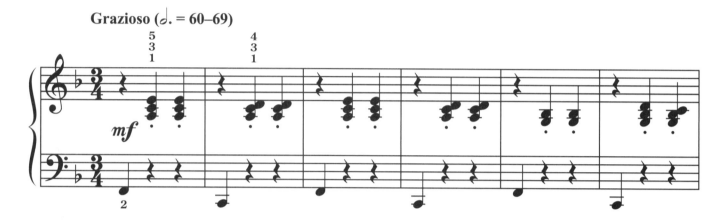

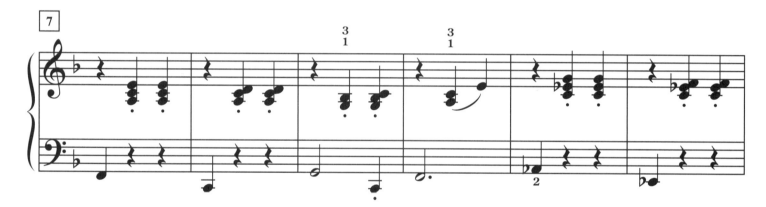

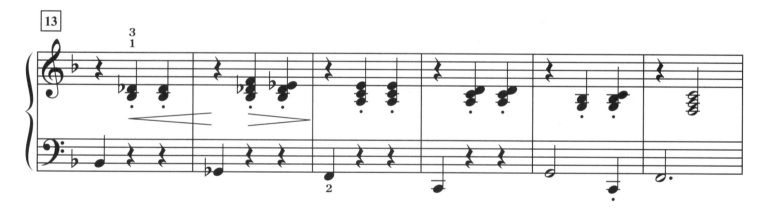

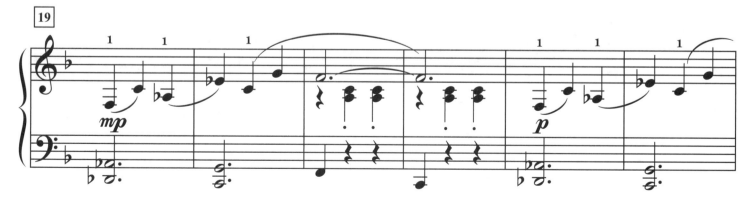

To Karen

THREE WALTZES
1.

PRIMO

Robert D. Vandall

2.

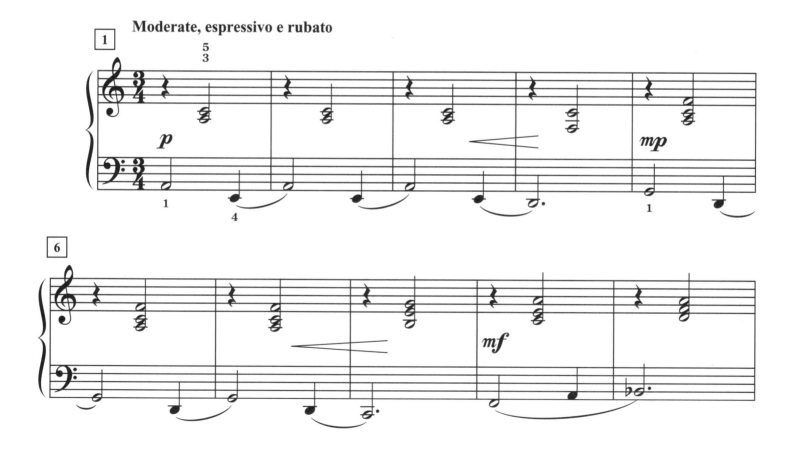

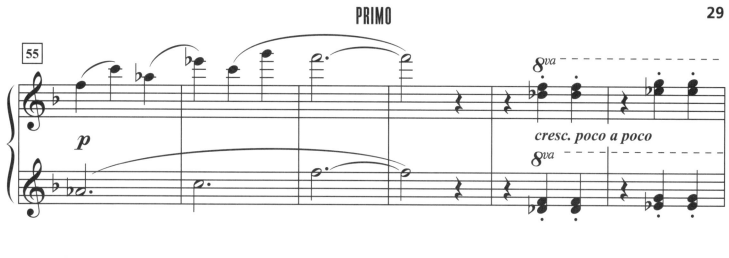

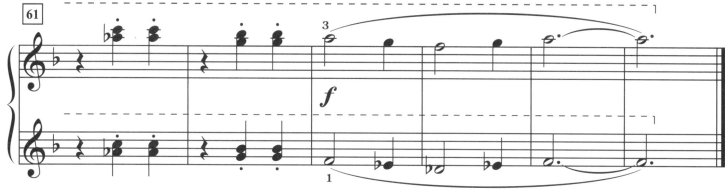

2.

Moderato, espressivo e rubato

3.

3.

For Carol Wickham

JAZZ DUETS

1.

SECONDO

Lucia Clarke

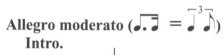
Allegro moderato
Intro.

For Carol Wickham

JAZZ DUETS

1.

PRIMO

Lucia Clarke

2.

SECONDO

2.

PRIMO

For Keith Wallingford

3.

SECONDO

For Keith Wallingford

3.

PRIMO

Commissioned by the Midland Michigan Music Teachers Association for its Keyboardfest 2001

THE GRAND FINALE

SECONDO

Catherine Rollin

Proud and uplifting, with great energy and vitality (♩ = 116–120)

Commissioned by the Midland Michigan Music Teachers Association for its Keyboardfest 2001

THE GRAND FINALE

PRIMO

Catherine Rollin

Proud and uplifting, with great energy and vitality (♩ = 116–120)

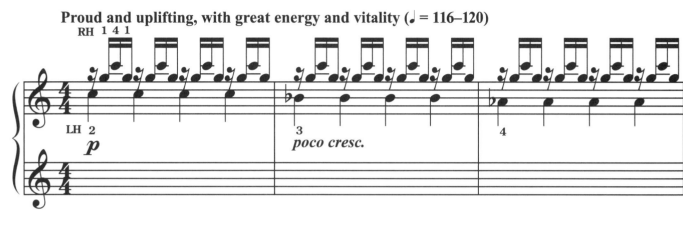

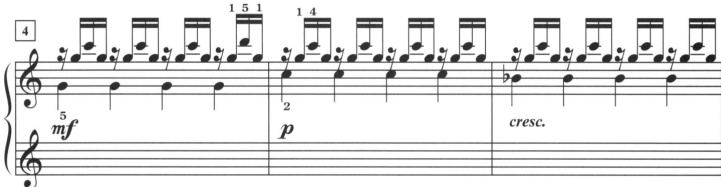

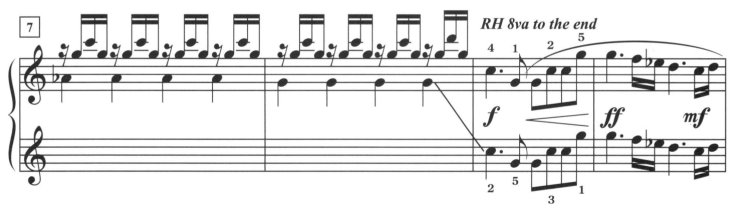

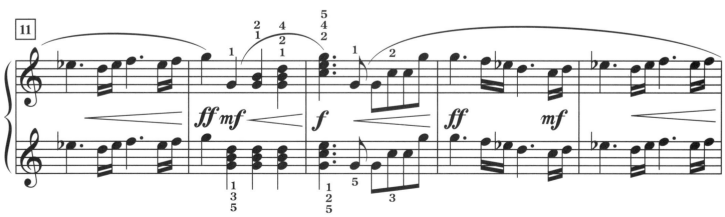

SECONDO

* The pedal will sustain the right hand in mm. 30–32 so that it can be lifted, allowing the left hand to play.

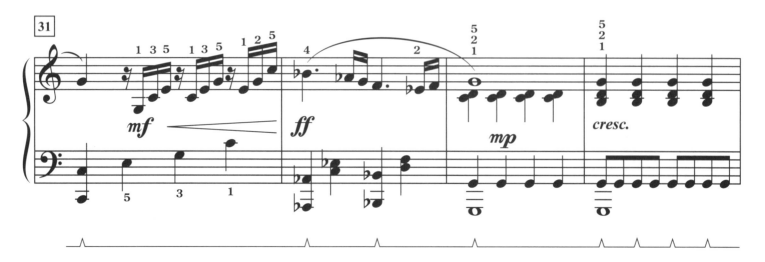

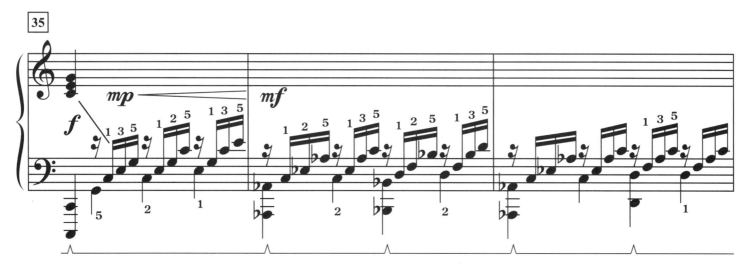

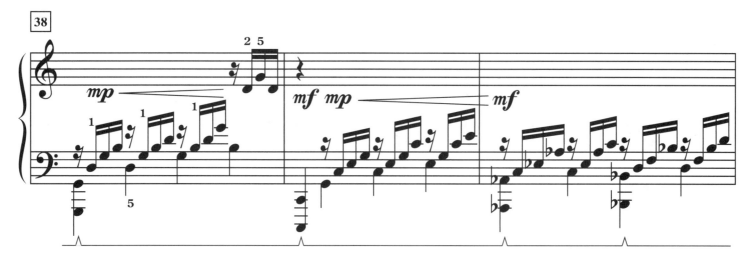

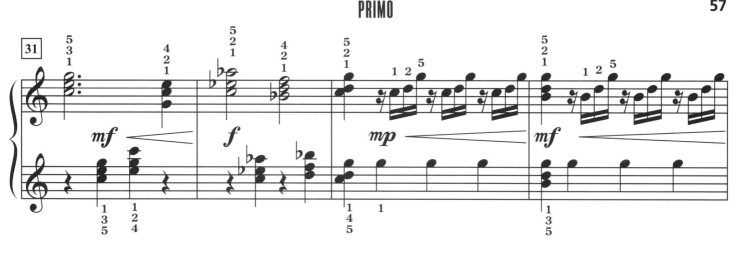

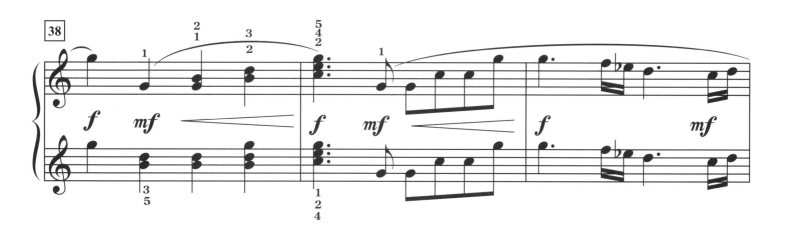

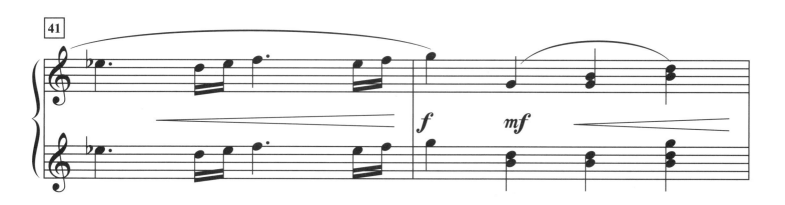

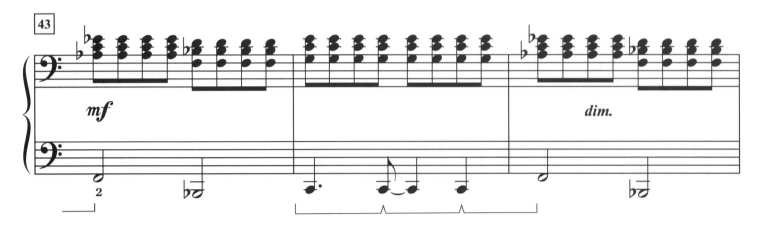

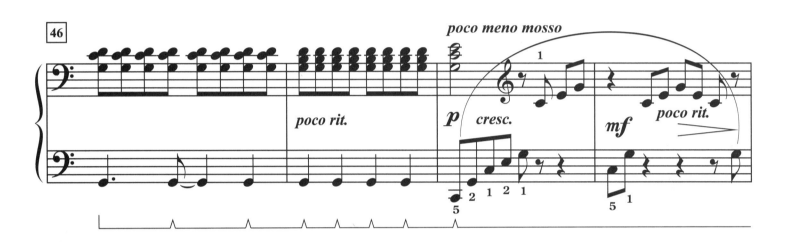

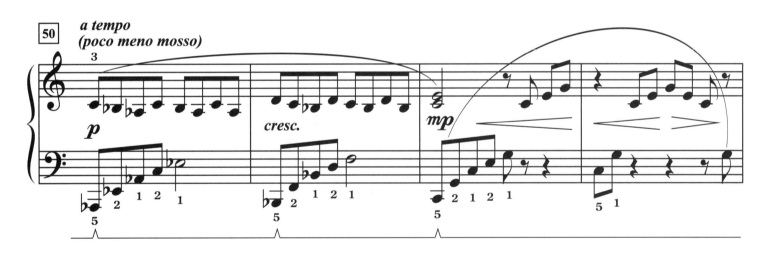

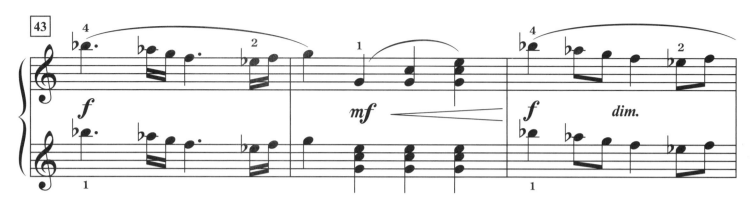

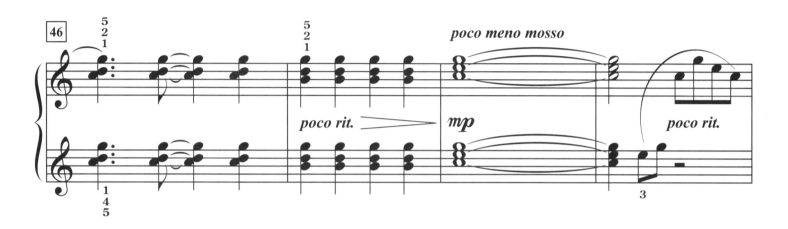

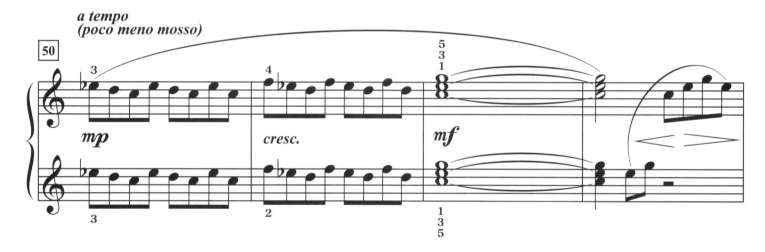

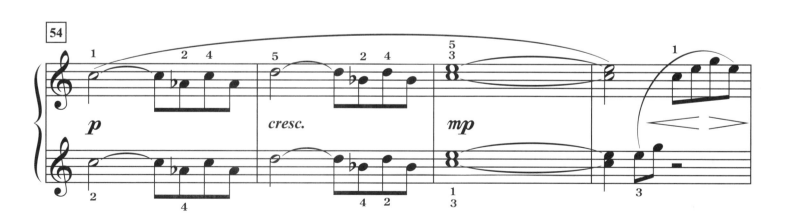

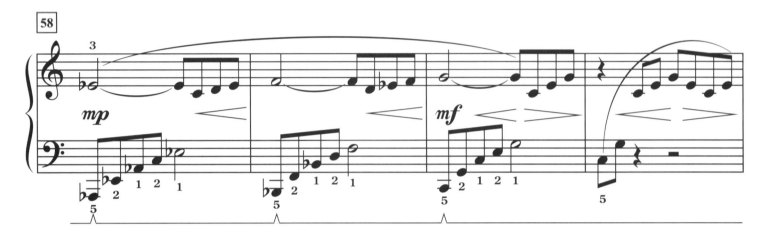

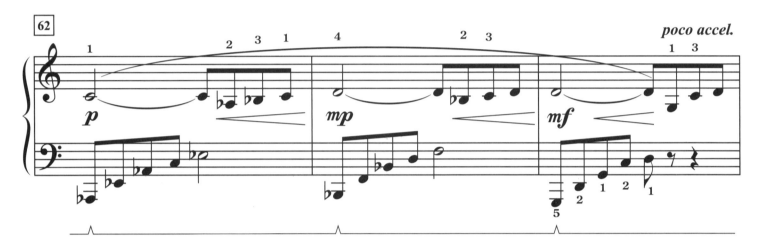

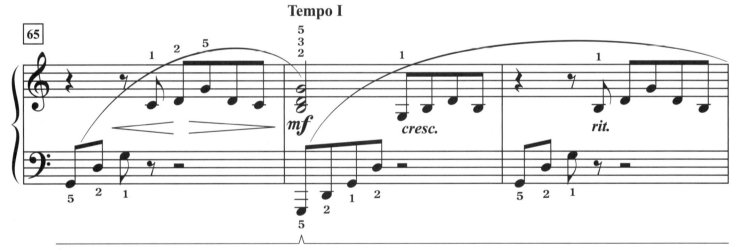

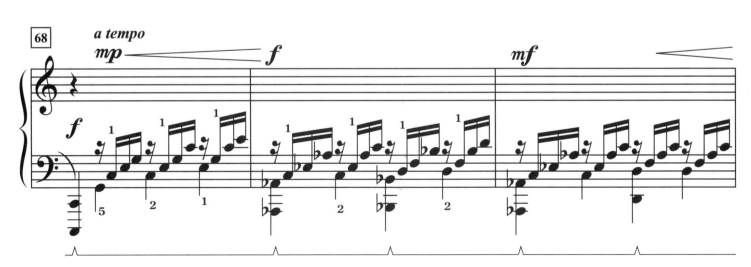

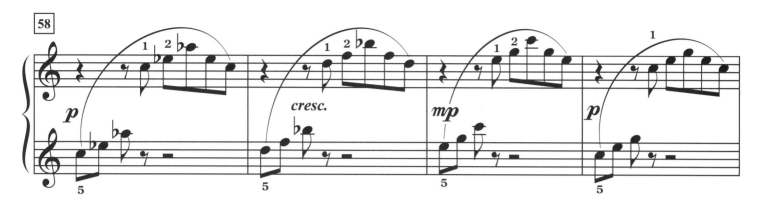

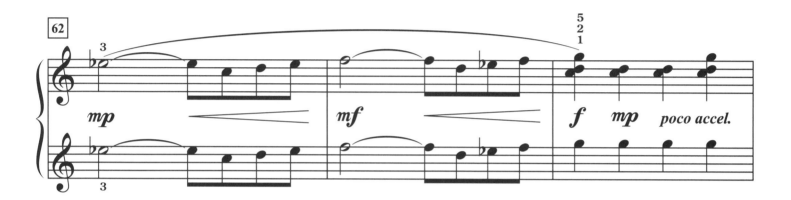

Tempo I

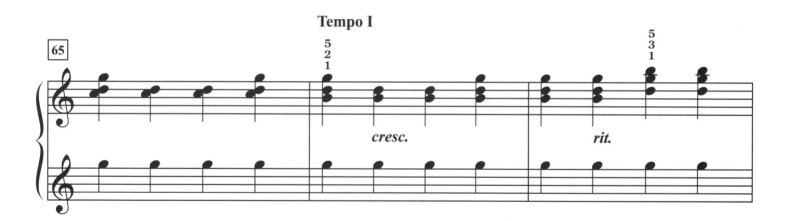

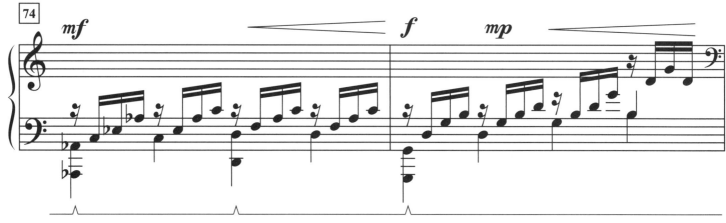

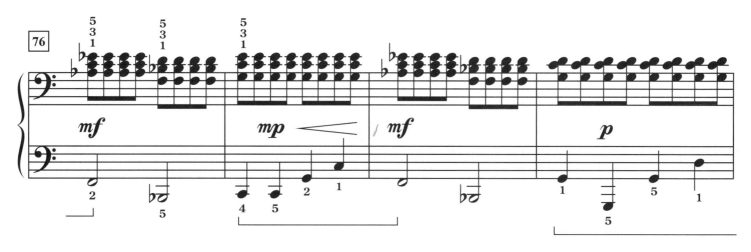

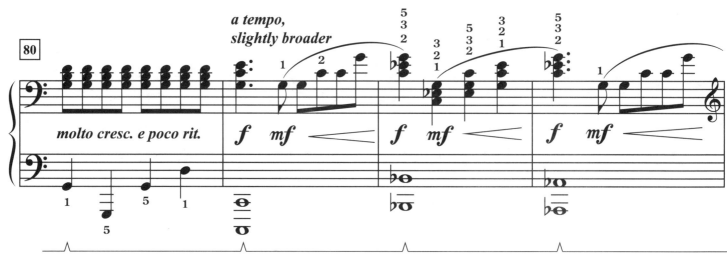

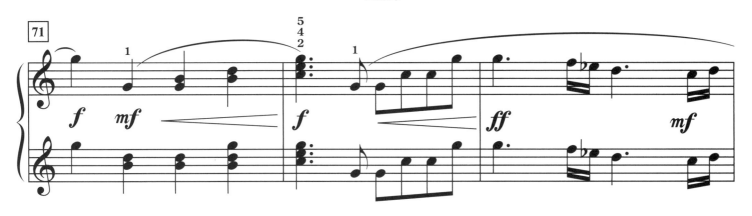

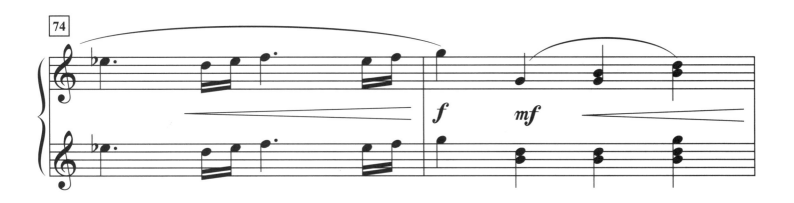

OSTINATO

SECONDO

Michael Shott
Op. 11, No. 8

Vivace

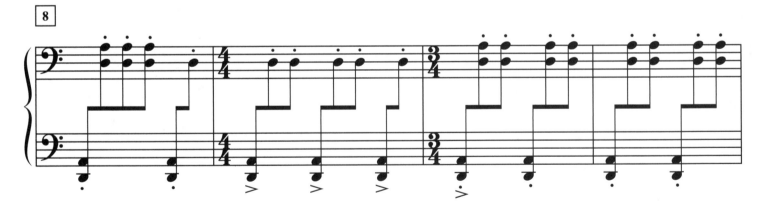

OSTINATO

PRIMO

Michael Shott
Op. 11, No. 8

16

20

24

28

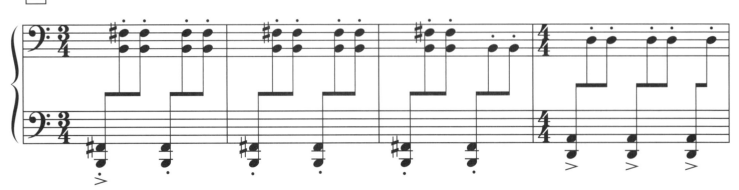

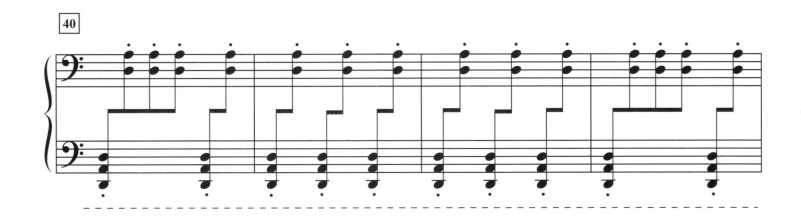